THE LIGHTER SIDE OF DEATH AND DIVORCE

And Legal Strategies For The Layman

To Smoothly Navigate Either

Margaret A. Jones

Printed in the United States of America

First Printing, 2015

ISBN: 069240533X
ISBN-13: 9780692405338
Fab4Girls Publishing

DEDICATION

To my Mom - Felicity Patricia – my biggest fan, to whom I owe my sense of humor. Although she passed away in 2013, before seeing my book published, I'm grateful for her command of the English language and her consistent assurance that each new chapter I dropped off at her house for her perusal was nothing short of brilliant.

CONTENTS

Dedication iii
Acknowledgments ix
Preface xi

BOOK ONE - DIVORCE

Introduction 3

1 Shock and Awe: Using A Divorce Coach To Help Sort Out Emotions 7

2 The War of the Roses: Surviving A High Conflict Divorce 13

3 Chattering Teeth: A Mediator's Perspective on Keeping A Sense Of Humor 18

4 Nice Mediations Gone Bad: Don't Screw Your Neighbor – Yet 23

5 I'll Keep Mine And We'll Share Yours: California Law At Its Finest 29

6 Is A Mediator Enough? Shouldn't I Have My Own Attorney? 33
7 Settle Now Or Settle Later: A Typical Litigated Case 38
8 Mediation: What To Expect 42
9 Collaborative Divorce: Another Option 48
10 Tips For A Successful Mediation 51
11 Premarital Agreements 56

The Lighter Side of Divorce 59

BOOK TWO – DEATH

Introduction 63

1 You Thought Death Was Scary? Facing Probate Can Be Downright Frightening 67
2 No Plan? Guess What, The State Will Create One For You! 72
3 We Do It For The Kids: Protecting Your Children's Inheritance 75
4 The AB Trust: Save Estate Taxes And Protect Your Spouse From Changing Your Beneficiaries After You Die 80
5 Let's Spend $30,000 Fighting Over A $30 Toaster 85

6 No One Can Love
My Kids Like I Do: Picking a Guardian
To Raise Your Bundles Of Joy 89

7 No One Can Love
My Money Like I Do: Picking the Lucky
Soul In Charge Of Your Children's Money 94

8 Free Forms: The Good, The Bad, And
The Ugly 99

The Lighter Side of Death 105

How To Pick A Good Attorney 107
Family Law 107
Estate Planning 108

Disclaimer 111

ACKNOWLEDGMENTS

I would like to thank my clients for their courage and wisdom - whether assisting them in preparing an estate plan or mediating their divorce - their ability to show up and do what it takes to get the job done is an inspiration to me always.

My two daughters, Caitlin and Jen, as well as my two stepdaughters, Brie and Tay, whom I love as my own, are a constant source of support, love and inspiration. My only hope is that when they decide to tie the knot I can convince them to do a prenup (unless of course the guy is filthy rich in which case they should cry uncontrollably at his mere mention of making *them* sign one).

I want to thank my editor and friend Bess Wiley without whose great writing suggestions, coupled with her belief that this book was more than just the silly little pamphlet I first envisioned, encouraged me to make it something worth reading.

I also need to acknowledge my ex-husband Richard, who taught me that divorce can be amicable. We are still friends to this day.

Last but not least, I am also grateful to my husband Vaughn, my sounding board and best friend. Even at the end of his longest days, he's never too tired to hear about mine.

PREFACE

When people ask me what I do for a living I often say: "Oh, I'm an attorney and my practice is in death and divorce. Are we having fun yet?" Because honestly, there is something to be said for keeping a sense of humor when your whole world is falling apart.

After years of practicing law and participating in a countless number of legal cases focused on estate planning and family law, I have gained much knowledge, experience, and hopefully, wisdom, when it comes to helping people get through these experiences and emerge whole on the other side.

I have found over the years, that many of the same issues and questions these intrepid warriors face on their journey come up again and again, and I thought it might be helpful to address these matters in a small but pithy resource in order to make the information available to anyone interested, while saving them my hourly rate! How fun is that!

This book, a snip-it of my world, will give the reader insight and information that I have gathered over my 24 years of writing clients' trusts and wills, helping them through the estate administration of a deceased family member, and dissolving marriages in the most amicable way possible. The names have been changed to protect the innocent, and where the stories are so unique that I felt a mere name change was perhaps insufficient to hide someone's identity, I have obtained their permission to publish their story. So rest assured, if you are a prospective OR new client of mine, you will not end up in my next book - unless of course you want to!

Death and divorce have a lot in common. Each is a great loss - possibly the worst thing anyone will ever face. Sometimes sudden. More often a long, drawn out but inevitable process. Always a huge unwelcome change. Nonetheless, this is the time to face a challenge head-on, overcome the loss, and to forge on with one's life in spite of either situation.

And of course, let's not forget the MONEY.

With divorce, the central question often is: "WHO GETS THE MONEY?"

And with death? No surprise, really. It's: "WHO GETS THE MONEY?"

Another thing death and divorce have in common is that, in most cases, both will require the help of an attorney at some point in the process. For many lucky people, it will be the first, and hopefully last, time they will ever need to consult an attorney.

However, whether for death or divorce, people now have to pay an arguably obscene hourly rate to a blood sucking, cold, heartless lawyer to navigate the oncoming hell.

I hate to deprecate my own kind here, but I'm just being realistic: we lawyers have less than a stellar reputation out there.

So, while you are in the midst of possibly one of the most hellish nightmares you'll ever go through in your lifetime, you'll have to rely on an attorney to help you get through it. And in the process, you'll have to face all of the ugly issues that come up when you are dealing with money - or lack thereof. This is definitely not for the faint of heart!

In any event, two things are certain: death is unavoidable and statistically, divorce isn't far behind.

Interestingly enough, the statistics on divorce in America are said to be higher than one would think, or what one may have heard. According to the 2009 U.S. Census, 46% of all marriages will end in divorce, a slight decline from the over 50% reported in earlier years. Much of this is attributable to the rise in cohabitation, longer periods of courtship before getting married, and rising median ages in couples before they take that fateful leap.

More good news: the Census also determined that within five years of divorce, 50% of men and 45% of women will remarry. And, even more – well – news: according to Psychology Today, 67% of second marriages and 73% of third marriages end in divorce!

(Can you say "PRENUP"?)

The statistics on death are less surprising. We know with 100% certainty that everyone, at some point in life, will die! Even so, the majority of people that I encounter have not done any kind of planning for this inevitable event. And, as you will see in these pages, a little planning will go a long way to ease the burden, financially and emotionally, for loved ones left behind.

Maybe you'll want to read this because you're in the middle of your own battle (estate planning and administration often have just as many war zones as divorce) or maybe because you're on the high dive ready to take the plunge to file for divorce, or finally get that living trust done.

Or maybe you'll want to read it because you can't remember the last time you got free legal advice! Whatever draws you, I hope you enjoy your ride through these pages. Learn a little. And most important, laugh a little. Because when it's all said and done, a little laughter never hurts, and keeping a sense of humor goes a long way in taking out the sting.

I know there are many resources available on these topics for anyone willing to take a look. Heck, when I get a call for legal advice outside my area of expertise even I will "Google it" and usually find a plethora of sound advice directly on point to my query. What I hope to offer with these pages is a little levity to an otherwise very grave subject (pardon the pun). In the immortal words of Mary Poppins, "Just a spoonful of sugar helps the medicine go down..."

And for those of you currently stuck in your own legal quagmire and less inclined to see any humor in it at all, I get it. And I apologize in advance if I seem overly sarcastic and irreverent. That's just my style and for whatever reason, my journey in writing this book seems to have exaggerated that side of me even more.

BOOK ONE - DIVORCE

INTRODUCTION

Crazy huh? Seems like just yesterday you were walking down the aisle at your wedding, ready to embark on the "happily-ever-after" of marriage with your dream mate. Odds against you, you nonetheless took the leap with a commitment to share the rest of your life together, forever, with this one person, through thick and thin, feast or famine, to always love with the same enthusiasm and exuberance you had the day you met. That's a lot to expect from even the most perfectly matched couple.

So, it didn't quite work out as you planned and now you've decided to go your separate ways. It's an emotional and difficult time to say the least. Men often see it as a failure, and woman just as a sad loss. The good news is that the legalities behind the split need not be the nightmare many people often hear about. More and more divorce attorneys are looking for better ways to cross the Ts and dot the I's without an ugly win/lose battle. In my own experience, I have met many colleagues, who, like myself, have opted out of representing clients in a litigated case and instead have limited their practice solely to mediation or collaborative law. My hope is that the trend continues and given the benefits I believe it will.

Although my family law practice is limited strictly to mediation, I did litigate in the first couple of years after law school, and learned a great deal during that time - much more than I wanted to, in fact. For those of you might not know the difference, a litigated case has two attorneys, each one representing one of the spouses in an attempt to come to an agreement regarding settlement of assets and support. In a mediated case, there is only one neutral mediator, usually a family law attorney, who represents the parties together in reaching a settlement. Occasionally, there are overlaps in these two approaches, which I will discuss more fully in my book.

Although the primary focus of the book is on mediated divorce, there is a lot of information on litigated cases as well. Often the best way to become informed about a better option is to learn about the problems and deficiencies with the alternative. Also, regardless of which path you choose - battling it out with lawyers in court or mediating a settlement - the law is the law and there is value in knowing what it is as you head down the primrose path of what you might think is your shiny newly "single" status.

It's my hope that anyone going through a divorce will read the entire section on divorce because, perhaps nestled into the advice in a chapter focusing on a topic you don't think is applicable in your case, there may be a bit of wisdom you can relate to and learn from. Even an amicable divorce can have moments of high conflict and even cordial couples can have times when all attempts of constructive communication fail.

Too afraid to get married after reading this book?! A quick word to the wise for those of you who have opted out of marriage and chosen instead to just live together: Please consider getting a cohabitation agreement. Although I haven't discussed these in my book, note that, after the Marvin v. Marvin case and its progeny, it's a very good idea to have such an agreement, if living in sin is your mode of relationship. Not that there's anything wrong with that.

My point is that if you think you are getting off scot free from potential liability by only living together and avoiding the whole marriage thing, you are sadly mistaken. At least if you live in California.

Although California abolished common law marriage in 1896, it does recognize cohabitation rights based in contract law, wherein oral, and even implied agreements, with your live-in soul mate apply. Those rights include asset awards as well as support. Even though the California courts ruled against Michelle "Marvin" (fun factoid: although they were never married, she legally took his surname after their breakup), the court's decision was clear, stating that these rights DO exist.

So beware, you rascals who "don't need a piece of paper to define your love. You nevertheless may want that piece of paper to protect it!

CHAPTER 1

SHOCK AND AWE: USING A DIVORCE COACH TO HELP SORT OUT EMOTIONS

More often than not, when couples come to me to mediate their divorce, one party will be in one emotional stage and the other party will be in another.

Isn't it funny how people in a lawsuit are referred to as "parties?" This has always seemed to me be one of the great, ironic misnomers. Because being a "party" to a lawsuit is probably the furthest thing from a "party" that one can imagine. But I digress.

As a reminder, for those of you who haven't been on the planet as long as the rest of us, the five stages typically experienced during any great loss, be it death, divorce or whatever, are: 1. Denial; 2. Anger; 3. Bargaining; 4. Depression; 5. Acceptance.

Oftentimes, how smoothly a divorce runs, greatly depends on which stage each spouse is experiencing. Identifying one's own stage as well as your spouse's can help you understand why he - or she - feels, or is acting, the way they are. And keeping this in mind can help tremendously in wading through the quagmire of emotions that typically come up.

A common theme among my mediations occurs when one party, let's say the wife, is already at the "acceptance" stage at the time we are starting the divorce, but the husband - always the last to know - is in the "denial" stage. She has already gone through all the stages at different points throughout the marriage, beginning at the time she told herself the marriage was probably over. She just failed to let her husband know then what was up.

So while the husband is blithely strolling through life, his unhappy wife has, either quickly or maybe over the course of years:

1. Denied her feelings;
2. Been very angry that she didn't get the fairy tale ending, because husband let her down, wasn't faithful, was bad with the kids, etc.

3. Tried to get him to change, via therapy or anything that might help save the marriage;
4. Given up and become resigned to being in an unhappy marriage;
5. Finally accepted that divorce is the only way out and is the right course of action for her to take.

Of course, the only thing husband hears is the closing act, where she tells him she wants a divorce. So he often feels, and rightly so, completely blind-sided by her revelation.

These are probably the most difficult cases to mediate, both emotionally and in the time required to negotiate a settlement. Husband, in this case, is still a bit of a deer in the headlights, and isn't really in an emotional place where he can negotiate who gets what, much less which days he will see the kids. So, in all his interactions with wife, whether in my office or outside of it, he's stuck with unresolved emotions in one of the earlier emotional stages of grief.

My first few such mediations were frustrating because, as the attorney, I wanted to get down to the business of figuring out a legal settlement that both parties were agreeable to.

But, in husband's quest for resolution and understanding, I had to switch gears from attorney to psychologist and somehow address his questions and conflicting emotions. At this point in the process, not only are husband and wife not getting the benefit of being helped by a trained therapist, but they are also doing so at a hefty hourly rate to their divorce lawyer. And let's face it. - Even the best family law attorneys know just enough about couple's therapy to be dangerous. So mediation becomes bogged down in make shift therapy sessions while the proverbial clock keeps ticking.

So, my advice?

Whether you are in the throes of a divorce, or even just thinking about doing so, identify the emotional stages that each of you are in, and use that knowledge to help shed light on, and gain a better understanding of, the underlying emotions you are feeling. Ideally, get some advice from a trained therapist. This is not to save the marriage necessarily, because I'm assuming here the marriage is over or you wouldn't be seeking a divorce. But a trained therapist can really help you get through the divorce.

One of my first mediations showed me the value of this first hand. A young couple with two small children hadn't been married long, so there wasn't a huge accumulation of assets during the marriage. They both worked and made about the same amount of income. I assumed they would settle relatively quickly, but after four or five sessions, we were still getting nowhere.

By then, they had spent maybe $1000 in attorneys fees over who was going to get the $20 toaster and who would get Tuesday night dinners with the children. My arsenal of conflict resolution tricks was running low. I even tried reasoning with them about the relative value of what they were fighting about, as compared to my fees to referee their battle.

All to no avail. The old "I'd rather give it to you than to him" was alive and well. And then, something magical happened. The next time they came to my office for another session, we settled the entire matter in about 30 minutes. After I wrote down all the terms of the settlement, the parties got up to leave. The wife stayed behind to use the restroom and I asked her what had happened. Why the sudden and huge shift in their ability to come to an agreement?

She said that in the time between their last session and the current one, they had gone to a therapist who was able to convince them that they should separate whatever emotions they were feeling towards each other from the legal issues that needed to be decided in the divorce. Duh. That's what I kept telling them over and over, but apparently the therapist was able to get the point across in a way that I couldn't. Or maybe they were just finally ready to listen. In any event, it made me a believer.

Today, the idea of getting professional help to facilitate a divorce has evolved, and there are now therapists that are specifically trained for this purpose. They are often called "Divorce Coaches" and can be a huge asset to the process. They can usually help a couple sort through all the emotional stuff - and believe me, there's lots of it - much better than an attorney or a family law mediator can.

My mediations, in which "high conflict" couples are also seeing a divorce coach, typically run the smoothest. This saves both husband and wife money, time, and emotional turmoil. It's true that the coaches aren't free, but the good ones can usually get the job done fairly quickly. And in the end you will save a bundle in attorneys' fees because the attorney/mediator time can now be focused on the legal issues, which is the reason you hired us in the first place.

CHAPTER 2

THE WAR OF THE ROSES: SURVIVING A HIGH CONFLICT DIVORCE

The universe was telling me something when my very first divorce case - when I still naively thought I was cut out for litigation - was something akin to that famous Michael Douglass and Kathleen Turner movie "The War of The Roses."

Funny to note that the ersatz "hero" in this film was actually the lawyer, played by Danny DeVito. He continually tried to stop his client Mr. Rose from engaging in toxic behavior toward his wife. When his attempts fail and they end up killing each other, DeVito becomes the narrator in the movie, compelled to tell their story in the hopes of warning other divorcing couples of what can happen when matters spiral out of control.

In any event, while many saw this movie as a tragedy at worst and dark comedy at best, I found it laugh out loud funny - much to the chagrin of my date at the time. I was laughing all the way through to the ending, when the love torn couple falls from the swinging crystal chandelier to their deaths. And especially so when Mrs. Rose, as they lay sprawled out on the marble slab foyer floor, with her last breath and every ounce of her flickering remaining life, gingerly reaches for her husband's hand, which has come to rest on her other wrist, picks it up and ... wait for it... tosses it aside! Tah stinkin dah! Ah, you just can't make this stuff up. Oh wait. I guess you can!

I never saw my date again – but no worries. I knew that out there somewhere, there were similarly warped single guys ripe for the picking.

I guess my thoughts of the grand humor of it all was foretelling of the kind of twisted personality I had that would eventually take me on my journey to become a family law attorney in the first place. Ah yes, to be in the middle of two people going through the demise of happily ever after - life doesn't get much better.

So, thinking this dubious plot would just never happen in real life, but knowing in my heart of hearts that reality is indeed stranger than fiction, I bring you back to my own personal War of the Roses, and, like Danny

DeVito, hope that my story will provide ye seekers of divorce a few pearls of wisdom.

Perhaps a little background about me is in order at this point. I started my practice in 1990 as an estate-planning attorney, in what was, at the time, the sleepy little town of Manhattan Beach. What this sleepy little burg has metamorphosed into since that time is the subject of a whole other book.

Be that as it may: the truncated version of my career path is that I opened my office. Moved my office. Moved again to an office where a divorce attorney who was leaving the area had her family law practice. She offered me her old desk, and her old phone number with the promise of her former clients as the start of expanding my estate planning practice to include divorce. Sounded innocuous enough. So I took a couple of intensive courses on family law to refresh my law school studies on the matter and waited by the phone.

Ring. Ring. Ring. The call came in, and on the other end of the line was a soft-spoken gentle voice of "Harry" asking if I could help him divorce his wife "Sally."

"As a matter of fact I can!" I beamed.

We scheduled our first meeting, during which I learned the facts of the case, and started him down the road to freedom. The problem? Neither he, nor Sally, were willing to move out of the house. And although it was actually Harry's separate property, until the Court awards it, neither party is required to leave.

So you see, now you have a divorcing couple, living together at the same time they are negotiating the terms of the divorce. Really? It's difficult enough to live with someone you want to live with, and have reasons to try and make it work... But to live with the enemy? The one whose cute little eccentricities have turned into annoying habits? The one who did you wrong, the one who let you down, and the one who took the best years of your life?

I'm not sure when things went really south and my memory of it is all a bit foggy, but I do remember a phone call about someone throwing furniture off the balcony. And that perhaps, even the police had been called. This was preceded days/weeks before, by Sally deliberately taking up smoking just to piss Harry off.

Harry would then run around the house opening up all the windows in the dead of winter to let the smoke out. Sally, not to be outdone, would follow in tow, cigarette in hand, slamming them closed. At this point, Harry saw fit to remove every window from its frame and stack them neatly in the basement below.

So there sat the happy couple, as I often envisioned it in my mind, at opposite ends of the couch, which was the only piece of furniture left in the house, on a cold winter night. Sally smoking. Harry coughing. Both freezing. And still, neither one willing to move out.

While one might think the moral of the story is: Move Out! In reality, and under California law, it's not that easy. Usually neither party can make the other move out, legally, that is. Even in Harry and Sally's case, where Harry owned the house as his separate property, he can't make Sally leave. Perhaps he could have if he could have proven to the court that Sally was abusive enough to warrant it.

But, of course, by the time you get a hearing and a ruling on the matter, the parties have already killed each other, or paid the attorneys so much money that now, neither one can afford to move out.

Until the court issues its Final Order regarding the division of assets - including who gets the house - both parties have the right to remain. In fact, the law goes even further and actually encourages the Harry/Sally scenario, in that legally, it's often not a good idea to move out pending the outcome of your case, even if you want to. From a strategic point of view, there can be advantages to staying in the family home, especially in cases where child custody is an issue.

So just because you think your divorce is, or will be, the worst hell ever, remember that you can help alleviate an all out battle by opting out of the win loose approach of a litigated case and instead choose mediation. You may be able to keep the windows and who knows, your wife may still have that accidental fall off the balcony.

CHAPTER 3

CHATTERING TEETH: A MEDIATOR'S PERSPECTIVE ON KEEPING A SENSE OF HUMOR

You know those little plastic wind-up toys? Well, one of my daughters gave me one that is a full set of teeth that chatters in a frenzy while randomly moving about. Can't help but chuckle when you see them - or so I thought. Anyway, I put them in my top desk drawer at some point after I began my mediation practice. My plan was to pull them out when clients digressed from the task at hand to an emotional battle of he said - she said. I thought: "What a great way to get back on track, ease the tension and insert some humor into the situation, all at the same time!"

Well, to this day I haven't had the nerve to pull them out.

I've had a lot of clients with great senses of humor, but somehow, when you are in the thick of it, it's difficult to see any humor at all. Best case scenario: I'd possibly end up wearing the teeth. Worst case, my clients would walk out.

Maybe I will pull the clattering teeth out during my last mediation before retiring. It may not be a high conflict case, but maybe a more cordial one. Maybe there might be a time when the wind-up teeth placed strategically in between the couple would be fitting and hopefully funny. Maybe not.

One mediation technique I had the gumption to try in one of my earlier mediations was one that I learned at a workshop. The seminar leader discussed different types of mediator styles, and the one that rang true for me was the "Teflon Mediator". It's really just like it sounds. You don't respond verbally. You don't feign sympathetic understanding. You don't offer suggestions to get them refocused. Whatever the clients throw at each other, or at you for that matter, just kind of slides off you as you maintain total equanimity in the face of emotional bedlam. Having mothered four teenage daughters through puberty, I've found this technique a virtual lifesaver in my personal life as well. That and white wine.

Anyway, the seminar leader went on to explain the clients will soon realize that their rants are having no effect, and are basically just wasting everyone's time, as well as their money. Sounds easy enough, right?

So there I was, in the midst of my representation of a high conflict couple. We had already spent a couple of sessions together and weren't really getting much done - at least in terms of negotiating a deal. They were getting *a lot* done as far as hurling insults, jabs, and accusations. Let's face it, you know this person inside and out, and once you start pushing buttons, the negative emotions can escalate pretty quickly and intensely.

So, I'm sitting there, and sitting there, and they just keep going at it as if I wasn't even in the room. So I tried several strategies I learned during role-playing in one of my continuing education seminars. Nothing was working.

Then I recalled from my arsenal of tricks that a Teflon Mediator, much like a mind-bending Ninja, could help get the point across that it's time to move on and get back to business. How? By appearing uninterested. So, I did.

When they both looked over at me while taking a break for oxygen, I subtly rolled my eyes to the side and then looked down at my watch. I guess I appeared a little too uninterested.

Because I did get a reaction, but it wasn't pretty. The wife looked over at me and contemptuously snarled: "Oh, are we *boring* you?!?!?"

I couldn't pull my manual out to look for an appropriate response so I just had to wing it. I can't recall my exact comeback, but I muttered something along the lines of "time, money and getting along" and sank back into my chair. I suppose you could say the "Teflon Ninja" approach worked on one level - because it made me the bad guy in their eyes instead of each other!

I have since learned how to refine the "Teflon Ninja" to help my clients move forward, because it often does help in the mediation process, but to this day the chattering teeth are still in the drawer. Although I must admit that in my imagination I've pulled them out on many occasions!

And then of course there are the divine mediations sent from above where the most egregious exchange is:

"You take the larger bank account, Honey."

" No, Pooky, I insist you take it."

Every once in awhile a couple comes along, and I just have to ask myself, "Why are these people divorcing? How is it that this marriage just didn't work?"

They are cordial, friendly, communicative, and generous to a fault in dividing up the assets. Even when it comes to sharing custody of the children, the discussions revolve around whose house will everybody go to for Christmas on even years, and whose house during odd years.

Perhaps these are the couples who are both at stage five in their stages of loss? The mediations are quick and painless. Short of my thinking that one or the other is being too nice, and may not have the capacity to look out for his/her own best interest -which is another chapter entirely - papers are signed and everyone goes their merry way - or unmarried way as the case may be!

I have no wisdom to impart with this last story with its fairy tale ending, just an observation. However, it does flow nicely as a segue to my next chapter, that being...

CHAPTER 4

NICE MEDIATIONS GONE BAD: DON'T SCREW YOUR NEIGHBOR - YET

Listen up, people.

If you are thinking of sleeping with the flirty neighbor or your spouse's best friend, or that attractive family friend you've always vehemently denied having feelings for - DON'T. Right?

At least not until the ink is dry on your divorce settlement.

You would think this is a no brainer, but I can't tell you the number of cordial mediations that have gone up in flames because one of the parties, during the middle of negotiations, decides to date, hang out with, hook up with, or sleep with someone who anyone with a soul or half a brain would consider off limits.

And of course, the other spouse ALWAYS FINDS OUT! They catch you in the act. They put the clues together. Some well-meaning friend, that you told in strict confidence, tells them. And of course, sometimes you will even blurt out a confession yourself - perhaps hoping it will assuage your guilt.

Because no matter how well the mediation is going, and no matter how close the parties are to reaching a fair settlement, when something like this happens, all bets are off.

Suddenly, any concessions one may have made in order to arrive at a settlement, any offers to help make the children's drop off time more workable, any rounding of bank account balances to make the numbers work - they are all now glaring instances of inequities that, according to the aggrieved party, must be readdressed. And, before that person is even in a place where he or she can talk division of assets or custody, we must first address the elephant in the room, and see if we can get the couple talking at all. So, common sense, I know, but DON'T DO IT! Not prudent, and arguably not nice either.

One nice mediation gone bad that comes to mind, was a young couple with a worker-bee husband, stay-at-home mom and three young children. Our sessions started out swimmingly. She was getting this, he was getting that, they would sell this, etc. Custody would be shared. All was good. Fortunately for them, they had a nice size estate, and he was a very successful businessman with a large steady income.

And then, the husband transgressed, succumbed to temptation, and slept with the wrong person, whom he was also sure was his next new Mrs. Right. Without going into detail, it was very upsetting to his wife, at which point the cordial negotiations spun off toward the dark side.

God Bless them, they stayed in mediation.

As a quick aside, my own personal statistic for success hovers around 97% for mediations in which a settlement is reached and the parties stay out of litigation. Even in some of my more brutal mediations, i.e. where revelations of infidelity are uncovered during the process, it's usually the case that whatever it was that brought the couples to mediation in the first place, keeps them there. Which is a good thing. Because it's the high conflict, high emotional cases that, when litigated, end up being the most costly, both monetarily and emotionally.

So, back to my story. Although this couple stayed in mediation, the tone changed dramatically.

In determining the spousal support amount, which had already been negotiated and agreed to, wife reassessed her situation and suddenly realized she had a much longer list of monthly necessities that she would need in order to maintain the standard of living she had grown accustomed to during the marriage. Necessities that had never been brought up during prior sessions. Husband, who had more than enough income to cover it, sat back and watched as the list and $$$ grew. Finally, wife felt she had included everything she could possibly need or want (and perhaps more). A monthly number was reached and a deal made. It was a relatively large settlement, commensurate with his salary and the life style to which she was accustomed. But that settlement was considerably more than the proposed support numbers contemplated merely a week before.

They had been married for over 10 years, a "long term" marriage by California law, and she was to receive the monthly support forever, or at least until he went back to court at some point and convinced a judge it was time to readdress things.

Soon after the divorce was final, I ran into wife at the grocery store. We chatted. (By the way, one of the perks of being a mediator instead of a litigator is that your clients still like you at the end of the process.) She mentioned to me that she was getting remarried. Imagine my surprise - all of that support, potentially a lifetime of substantial monthly payments, gone.

I couldn't believe she would give up the amount of money that she had fought so hard to get. I told her: "You know your support payments will forever go away?" Her response? "Oh I know. It was never about the money for me. But it was for him and I just wanted to get him where it hurts. Payback's a mother#$#$&$#!

Speaking of transgressions: There is the arguably even uglier scenario of having to make spousal support payments to your ex wife and her new room mate, your ex good friend, who single-handedly was responsible for breaking up your marriage in the first place..

Regardless, now you ask in total disbelief and amazement: "She slept with my best friend and now I have to pay her alimony?" Yep. Best to just try and get over it. California divorce is no-fault. That means that no matter what one party did to the other, community property is divided 50/50, child support is a formula and spousal support is a mish mash of statutory factors, none of which has to do with infidelity.

There are certain transgressions that may have an impact on the outcome. Murder, for instance. But for the most part, you could end up writing a monthly check to your ex-wife, who is now living with your ex best friend, to support them in their new happy home for quite some time into the future.

Because you see, before California became a "no fault" state – under a law signed by Ronald Reagan in 1970 - divorces were even uglier. I know, hard to believe. In order to get divorced, you had to prove that one party was at fault -infidelity and cruelty typically topped the top ten reasons. Perjury abounded, even fabricated stories made up by the husband and wife in collusion.

Couples often developed legal fictions, elaborate schemes as it were, with accompanying testimony, as to why they deserved to sever their union. So in many, if not most cases, where the couples just wanted out, they had to make up stuff in order to do so. Horrible stuff that became part of the court record. So you see, ultimately the no-fault law was really a good thing.

Of course, like any good thing, the wrong set of facts can become a bad, bad thing - like the ex who pays alimony to her husband after catching him in bed with his brother's wife.

In any event, finding fault is no longer a requirement, and couples in California can now go their separate ways based on "irreconcilable differences" or "incurable insanity." That second option usually gets a chuckle out of my clients when we are filling out the initial Petition together. See? Divorce can be fun!

CHAPTER 5
I'LL KEEP MINE AND WE'LL SHARE YOURS: CALIFORNIA LAW AT ITS FINEST

I often see the following scenario in my mediations: couples who come to me saying that they have already worked everything out, and they just need me to draw up the agreement and file the paper work. Sounds easy enough, doesn't it?

Not always.

The problem is that oftentimes their potential agreement has no basis in California law - unless by chance, it does. More often than not, when they draw it up themselves, what they may have thought seemed fair when they sat down and talked about it, in fact will not hold up legally. Because, you see, sometimes the law just isn't fair. Shocking, I know.

Like Bob and Carol who came to me with everything worked out. They only had two major assets: a retirement account, and a brokerage account. Each was worth about $200K. The plan was that he would keep his retirement account, and she would keep the brokerage account. The contents of the brokerage account were solely an inheritance to her from her mother. They were able to keep it untouched while they lived off of his income.

Seems fair enough - except under California law, her inheritance is her separate property, so she is entitled to a 100% of it. Whereas his retirement, accumulated during the marriage, is community property. So she gets 50% of that as well. Oops.

And then there's another relatively common scenario.

Ted already owns a condo when he marries Alice. During the marriage, he keeps the title in his name and earns a nice income from renting it out. The rent it generates is more than enough to cover the mortgage payments and other expenses. Every month, Ted deposits the rent checks into his separate checking account, into which he also deposits his paychecks. From this same account, he makes the Condo's mortgage payments. Alice owns the family residence that they live in, which has no mortgage. She is not employed. Ted makes enough that she doesn't have to work. Ted pays all the bills and they enjoy a nice life in which they travel extensively and live quite well.

Years later, they decide to divorce and after a few friendly discussions, they decide that Alice will keep her house and Ted will keep his Condo, which he has now paid off. Seems fair enough, right? Guess again.

Under California law, his salary is community property, i.e. half hers. And so is anything they've used the salary to acquire. Even though the Condo was always titled in his name, the mortgage payments used to pay down the principal, i.e. acquire it, were made from an account where he deposited his salary - community property. So now wife has an interest in his Condo. And husband may have to pay a forensic accountant a large sum of money to determine what her share is of the property.

Had he taken the Condo rent, which is his separate property, and put it into an account that didn't have his salary in it and then made the mortgage payments from this account, she would not have acquired an interest in the Condo. Is that fair? Arguably not.

But now it's my job to let the happy couple know these facts. Unlike some litigation attorneys, my mouth does not start salivating and I don't start rubbing my hands together at the prospect of the ensuing battle. However, the couple does need to know the legalities of their proposed settlement. It's my job to inform them and it's what they are paying me for. They are relying on my expertise in the area of family law to guide them in terms of what the law is and what their rights are.

Sometimes when such legalities are revealed, a couple will choose to stick with the original plan. But often, one party, usually the one who gave up more than he/she needed to, wants to throw out their Plan A and take a bigger piece of the proverbial pie. At which point, the tone of the mediation can turn a bit sour. But hey, there is no good or bad guy here - except maybe me for delivering the bad news.

Note that, as their mediator, I am only concerned that before they reach a final settlement, they know what the law is and understand their rights. If they want to go with Plan A, I will not stop them - nor will the judge who ultimately signs off on their agreement. The judge doesn't care if a couple's agreement is fair or reflects the law. As long as the I's are dotted, the T's are crossed, asset/income disclosures are made, and the right forms are filled out correctly (no easy task), then all's good.

CHAPTER 6

IS A MEDIATOR ENOUGH? SHOULDN'T I HAVE MY OWN ATTORNEY?

In litigation, each spouse has the benefit of having their own advocate look out for their best interest. Not only do you have someone to fight for you and what you may be entitled to, but you can also be sure you won't be taken advantage of by an overbearing spouse. The warm and fuzzy feeling of having your own attorney can help alleviate possible fears that you won't get your desired outcome.

I can't believe I have "warm and fuzzy" in the same sentence as "attorney."

Sounds good, yes? Unfortunately, the benefits of having your own attorney are often overshadowed by the disadvantages of allowing third parties - the attorneys and the judge - determine the outcome of your case. The adversarial game between lawyers is just that: a game, with a winner and a loser. What the parties want is often secondary. While the lawyers do their posturing and fight for the best possible outcome for their clients, the clients are being dragged along for the bumpy ride.

For the most part, they are powerless to step in, put things in perspective, and perhaps step on the brakes, until of course their retainers are used up, at which point the lawyers typically back off and miraculously settle. Clients trust that their lawyers know what's right and are doing what's best for them. They freely give away this power because of their uncertainty with the law and the process. As a result, lawyers are left to run amock, entwined in ongoing battles, wasting time and their clients' hard-earned money.

If you have decided to pursue your divorce through mediation, whether or not you consult with an attorney during the process, is usually a choice left up to you to make. For the majority of my own mediations, we do not get attorneys involved at all. As a family law attorney, I am familiar with the law and believe that an in-depth discussion of it is an integral part of the process in determining the outcome of any case. How can a party know what may or may not be fair without knowing what he would be entitled to under the law? As I mentioned earlier, a settlement agreement is not limited to only reflecting what is fair under the law.

There are several ways attorneys can be involved in the mediation process. Some clients will retain their own attorney from the get-go. They want to periodically check in with their own advocate to let them know what's being discussed and get their opinion about it. Other times, the parties will proceed without attorneys and then perhaps consult with one in regards to one particular issue.

For those clients who have not consulted with an attorney at any point in the negotiations, they may consult with one prior to signing the final agreement and submitting it to the court. I always advise these clients to have their own advocate review the agreement on their behalf, so that they are comfortable with their understanding of the law and the terms of their settlement.

To date, I have yet to have a mediation break down upon a final attorney review. In my experience, by the time the clients sign the final agreement, they know exactly what they are signing and all the legal ramifications. If they have agreed to something that deviates greatly from what the law would otherwise dictate, I make sure they know it so that by the time their attorney gets involved there are no surprises.

Some clients are hesitant to mediate their divorce without having their own attorney because of power struggles in the relationship. They fear they will be unable to stand up for what they want or need and without the aid of an attorney to do it for them. They fear hey will not be able to negotiate a fair settlement. A good mediator pays close attention to the power balance between the spouses and uses specific techniques to address any imbalance. In fact, this is really the primary job of the mediator, as I see it: to help each party negotiate his or her own best deal. If one party is afraid to assert him or herself, how can they possibly negotiate a fair settlement? As a neutral third party, I will even occasionally take sides during negotiations, if I feel that it's warranted. By doing so, I can keep a level playing field, so that neither party can take advantage of the other.

In a very small handful of cases, my assistance in this regard isn't enough. Although the parties may have reached a settlement, I'm not comfortable that one of the parties has really had the ability to look out for his best interest, even with my help. When this happens, I will insist that that party consult with their own attorney before signing the final agreement. This not only protects the spouse who may be unwittingly giving away the farm, it also protects the integrity of the agreement. If each party consults with their own attorney in a case like this, it's much more difficult to come back later on to set aside the agreement claiming undue influence.

If you do decide to retain an attorney during divorce mediation, you should keep in mind a few things.

Lawyers who understand and support mediation can help mediating spouses in several ways: by informing them of their legal rights and options, by coaching them throughout the negotiations, and even by coming up with creative settlement ideas. Most consulting lawyers charge a reasonable hourly fee and don't require a large retainer or advance deposit. A spouse pays for only as much consulting time as is needed.

That being said, divorce mediation is still a relatively new way of approaching divorce. Many adversarial lawyers have little or no experience with the non-adversarial approach used in mediation. Some even disapprove of mediation, arguing that divorcing spouses should not negotiate on their own, but only through lawyers. These attitudes are slowly changing, as divorce lawyers become more aware of mediation and its benefits for their clients. Meanwhile, spouses wishing to mediate their divorce need to find consulting lawyers who are "mediation-friendly."

CHAPTER 7

SETTLE NOW OR SETTLE LATER: A TYPICAL LITIGATED CASE

Sooner or later, odds are you will probably settle. On average, 93% of all litigated family law cases settle before trial. Some will settle early and many will settle on the eve of trial.

My experience shows that a typical scenario is as follows: Dick retains his attorney and Jane retains hers. Dick meets with his attorney who soon after files the initial Petition for Dissolution. Dick's attorney gets a general idea of the couple's finances and marital story and then informs Dick that yes, he could get the house, the kids, and pay little or no alimony. Blah, blah, blah.

Meanwhile, Jane is meeting across town in the fancy high-rise firm with her team of lawyers. Her lawyer is undoubtedly making similar suggestions that she will be the victor, probably get just about everything she wants – and that Dick will end up paying her attorneys' fees. Jane signs her fee agreement, files her Response, retainers are paid, and GAME ON.

Then begins the litigation phase known as "discovery." Basically, I'll show you mine if you show me yours. If only it were that easy! Actually, there is a mandatory set of forms that the parties must exchange that list all known assets and debts, as well as current income and expense numbers. Although short (a few pages each) they are comprehensive and signed under penalty of perjury. If an asset is left off or income understated, then any subsequent agreement reached by the parties can be set aside on grounds of fraud. But many attorneys believe that in most cases these forms are insufficient, and instead they pull out their arsenal of discovery tools to get to the meat of the case. Interrogatories are served, depositions are scheduled, and motions and court hearings are set.

Eventually the discovery phase is done and Dick and Jane's attorneys have all the information they need to proceed to trial. Dick and Jane by the way really have little or no control over any of this. They trust their attorneys are acting in their best interests and doing what they need to do, so they just sit back and watch as the fees escalate and the retainers are used up.

And then?

Dick's attorney tells him that after looking at all the evidence, he really is only entitled to XYZ. Cross-town, Jane's attorney tells her, that after looking at all the evidence, she really is only entitled to XYZ and then guess what: Yep, the parties settle and get XYZ. The lawyers are the heroes because they settled the case before trial. And Dick and Jane never know what hit them.

Because you see, by that time the lawyers have made a good chunk of money and if they go to court with a case that really has no business being in court, two things can happen. One, they can loose. Lawyers hate to loose. Or Two, they piss the judge off for wasting his time on something that should have settled long ago. And trust me. You don't want to piss off the judge.

My second litigated case was a good example of the discovery phase gone badly. It went something like this. He was a bank teller. She was a waitress. They had one young child, did not own their home or any assets to speak of, and had been married only a few years. I filed the Petition and her attorney filed a Response. Nothing to divide really, no custody battle. A couple of weeks later I received a stack of interrogatories from her attorney three inches high. I exaggerate - not.

Interrogatories are written questions regarding assets, income, businesses (none here) etc. Now, in the name of advocacy, I am supposed to reply with my own set of documents as well, and challenge as many questions as possible by refusing to answer them on various grounds. Then, opposing counsel floods me with more documents in response and so on. Oftentimes, the lawyers can end up in court asking the judge to decide if even a certain question must be answered.

Can you imagine how much lawyer time - and client money - has been spent by this point, and we haven't even gotten to actually answering the question?

Well, in my naivety, I phoned her lawyer upon receipt of this first set of redundant, unnecessary and superfluous questions and asked him why the deluge of documents. Did he think my client was hiding something? Their salaries were barely enough to cover the rent. There wasn't even anything to divide. His response was that he hadn't really looked closely at the case and that this was the standard procedure for his office in all cases. Really? I asked him to take a look at the case, and see if he still thought this was necessary and can't we save these kids some money on attorney's fees?

That got a resounding "No," at which point I was forced to respond with my own set of documents... and away we go.

Do the math, people! Settle now. Or settle later and end up with the same terms but with a lot less money in your pocket.

CHAPTER 8
MEDIATION: WHAT TO EXPECT

A good divorce mediator should be a family law attorney, because you will probably be spending most of the time in mediation discussing the law. My first family law mediation course, back in the early 90's, consisted of a group of about 25 students. About half of us were divorce attorneys, and the other half were therapists seeking to expand their practice to include divorce mediations.

Oddly enough, there was also one general contractor. He said he had so many jobs go wrong because at some point during the construction, the husband and wife decided to call it quits. Not just the house building/

remodeling but the marriage as well! The contractor was hoping that the seminar would teach him how to keep the couple happily married long enough so that he could finish the job and get paid!

Most, if not all, of the therapists stuck it out, but many of them that I spoke with at the end of the week-long course all had the same comment. They didn't feel they had the requisite legal knowledge to help a divorcing couple negotiate an agreement. Although they had the skills to deal with any conflict that may have come up, they weren't equipped to give guidance about the actual terms of a settlement in light of the law. They realized that the clients would probably have to consult with attorneys throughout the process so they would be better served by just having a knowledgeable family law attorney as their mediator.

Some of the therapists planned to team up with a family law attorney and do the sessions together. This may make sense for very high conflict cases, but it seems to me that a lot of money may be spent unnecessarily for the typical mediation where the couple can work through their differences well enough for meetings to be productive, and agreements to be reached. I'm guessing most clients would not want to pay a therapist to sit in on every meeting if they aren't really needed. That being said, there are times in a mediation, when therapists are badly needed and can be very helpful.

So, you've found a good family law attorney to serve as your mediator. Now what? Set out some ground rules. One important rule is whether or not there will be full disclosure. That is, whether any communication between only two of you must be fully disclosed to the other. I prefer this... I think it's in keeping with the spirit of the mediation. The other option - that communications asked to be kept private will be kept private - is fine as well. The important thing is that everyone knows the rules up front so there are no surprises.

If you decide on full disclosure, please don't call your mediator on the phone and begin the conversation with "Don't tell my wife, but..." Usually I can cut the client off before they spill whatever confidence it was they wanted to share, but if I can't it may end up creating a bit of a situation.

High conflict cases may require lots of rules. Let the other person speak. Don't hurl insults. Don't hit the mediator. You know, the normal stuff.

You will also want to make sure the mediator has a fairly comprehensive fee agreement in place. It should not only address his or her hourly rate and retainer - hopefully refundable - but should also include such tidbits as the use of outside experts, the legal ramifications of any agreements reached, and what happens in the event the mediation is not successful and the parties end up in litigation i.e. can they use any part evidence gathered in the mediation for their trial.

With the logistics out of the way, you should now be ready for your first session. Oftentimes we will begin by filling out the initial Petition for Dissolution. Your mediator should be a one-stop shop. She should be able to complete and file all the necessary paperwork required by the court, as well as help you negotiate the terms of your settlement.

Many clients like to get the Petition filed right away, because once the Petition is served on the other party, the minimum six-month waiting period required by California law before the divorce can be finalized starts to run. Not that they're in any hurry or anything.

Some clients will prefer to wait before filing the Petition. They want to see how the mediation progresses before they are ready to commit with the Petition and its legal ramifications.

At this point, I will usually start by getting a general idea of their assets, as well as when and how they were acquired. Once this is determined, I can give them an idea of the nature of the property, i.e. community, separate or mixed, and how it should be valued. This, in turn, usually leads to a discussion about the law.

Oftentimes I will have a couple who, once armed with an understanding of California law, can discuss their wishes with each other outside of mediation. They come back with tentative agreements, which we then all discuss and tweak, if necessary. My purpose at that point is merely to make sure their understanding of the law is accurate, so that any decisions they've made are based on correct information. I can also help by offering creative solutions that they may not have considered. This will sometimes be the case with the family residence, where neither can afford to buy the other out, but they want to keep it in the family long enough for their children to live in through the end of high school.

In marriages where there are commingled assets, which have both community and separate property components, we discuss how the law would determine values. In some cases, the parties will agree to retain a neutral expert to do a valuation. We also may employ experts for other valuations, i.e. for a business or a pension plan. The advantage of the couple jointly hiring a neutral expert is that they can get an honest opinion, and use that information in the mediation when negotiating their final agreement.

In a litigated case, typically each party would hire their own expert, for thousands of dollars each, who would skew the facts and results as much as possible to favor his/her client. They would then battle it out in court and let the judge decide whom he likes better. Can you say "cha ching"?

In cases where there are minor children, we will of course discuss child support, custody, and visitation. And in cases where there is a disparity in income, we will discuss spousal support. Sometimes, it will take awhile to gather all the data necessary to determine the amount that should be paid for spousal support. If a party needs support payments right away, while we are figuring out what the ultimate amount will be, we will discuss temporary payments to be paid in the meantime. Temporary payment amounts are usually determined by a very simple formula. If the party receiving the payments wants the added protection of the court, pending the filing of their Final Stipulated Judgment, I can prepare a Stipulation and Order for Temporary Support that we can file in their case.

In litigation, the parties' attorneys will oftentimes battle out even these temporary support amounts and obligations.

Once we've gathered all the information we need, discussed the law, as well as the underlying interests, concerns and desires of each party, we work together to find an agreement that everyone is happy with - or, hopefully, at least not really pissed off about.

When there are impasses, an experienced family law mediator is usually able to employ certain skills to move past them, so the parties can still reach an amicable settlement. Ultimately, however, the parties must agree. It is not the mediator's job to decide for them, which is actually what makes mediation so powerful.

In a litigated case, whenever you let a judge decide the outcome of your case, who knows what you may end up with? You might catch him on a good day - for you - and win big. But you might also loose big. Or, you may end up with what you should have settled for in the beginning, what was fair under the law. Why take that chance when you don't have to. Remember, even if you do win big, look at what it took to get there. What it cost you in stress, in your relationship with the other party, and even in attorneys' fees.

CHAPTER 9
COLLABORATIVE DIVORCE: ANOTHER OPTION

For those of you who just can't get past the idea that the best resolution to your divorce can only be reached by two attorneys battling out your case for you, there is still another option to a fully litigated case: a process called Collaborative Law.

In a collaborative case, both parties and their attorneys enter into an agreement that focuses on employing cooperative techniques rather than adversarial strategies and litigation. Probably the most important component of the collaborative agreement is that if a settlement is not reached, the attorneys must withdraw from the process and allow new attorneys to participate in the ensuing litigation. Wow, what a concept! A method that actually discourages the attorney's motivation to drag out the case in protracted litigation.

Another important feature of the collaborative case is that the parties and attorneys engage in four-way meetings that help keep the parties empowered in the process. So much of a typical litigated case is time spent with the attorneys talking only to each other without the parties present. All the while the clock is ticking and the fees are climbing.

Also, the "discovery phase" is tempered from the formal, expensive, time consuming one that I warned you about in chapter seven on litigation. In case it was so gruesome you've chosen to forget, it involves needless depositions, court hearings, motions, subpoenas, etc to gather information that each party is entitled to, and that could just be handed over freely, without all the cost, to one that is more similar to what is typically done in mediation.

Attorneys that practice collaborative family law usually have a cadre of other professionals that they team up with to help when needed, including divorce coaches, forensic accountants who specialize in family law, therapists where child custody issues exist and even financial coaches to help the parties find creative solutions to optimize investment goals. Depending on the nature of the assets and circumstances involved in a dissolution, some, all or none of these professionals can be consulted as the parties see fit.

I have participated as a collaborative attorney in the past and will continue to do so in the future, although I still believe that, when possible, mediation is the best way to go. Mediation has all the benefits of a collaborative case, including the employment of attorneys if needed. But in my experience, mediation still saves the clients' time and money in most cases.

CHAPTER 10

TIPS FOR A SUCCESSFUL MEDIATION

It's hard to imagine a more difficult time than when one is going through a divorce. On an emotional level, a range of emotions are experienced - betrayal, anger, disappointment, sadness, fear, hopelessness and revenge. From a financial perspective, divorce involves almost every aspect of one's financial life. A divorce involves a division of marital property including one's home, pensions, bank account, inheritances, and even personal property. Divorce also involves making decisions about health insurance, life insurance and financial security.

And don't forget spousal support. The possibility to be forever tied to your ex-spouse for an amount based on a host of rules couched in a lot of discretionary and gray areas in determining what will be paid, and for how long.

Finally, and probably most importantly, during a divorce, decisions need to be made about the children, their parenting schedules, education, health and support.

Unfortunately, most people did not have formal conflict resolution training growing up. As such, for the vast majority of people, conflict is handled in two ways: ignore it or attack.

This is not just cultural. To a great extent we are hardwired to have "fight or flight" responses. Thus, to address conflict head-on in a non-adversarial manner is counter-intuitive. Mediation provides clients with a safe venue to discuss their divorce. Mediation however will not automatically undo years of ingrained behavior. Mediators and therapists can offer tools to their clients that will help them prepare mentally and emotionally for the divorce process. Below are a few suggestions.

1. Recognize your own attitude towards conflict.

   Ask yourself these questions:

   When I am faced with conflict, what do I feel?

   When I was growing up, how did people in my family usually resolve conflict?

What is my usual method for dealing with conflict? Knowing how you feel about conflict is the first step towards being able to handle it effectively. If you know you are conflict-avoidant, this awareness can be very helpful in assessing how the mediation is going. Are you agreeing because you really agree or because you want to avoid conflict?

2. Normalize conflict.

Conflict is not only natural, but also inevitable. There is no creativity without conflict. The act of questioning the status quo is a way to come up with creative alternates. Often, clients come into mediation thinking that in order to mediate they must agree on everything. Mediation, however, is the time to discuss areas of disagreement. It would not be helpful for a client to avoid addressing a conflict at mediation only to realize later that he/she has made a mistake and therefore regret a decision later on.

3. Conflict as opportunity

It is often conflict that leads to transformative moments in mediation when, for example, one party apologizes or acknowledges something important. Conflict leads to dialogue, and it is through dialogue that the parties can become more enlightened about a particular issue. Discussions that skirt the real issue or avoid conflict are not true or full discussions. In the right setting, addressing conflict has an enormous potential for positive results.

4. Listening

THE MOST IMPORTANT ASPECT OF A SUCCESSFUL MEDIATION IS TO LISTEN TO YOUR SPOUSE. In fact, this is the most important aspect of any discussion where conflict is involved. Think about what happens when you are involved in an argument. You make your argument and the other person responds. Typically at this point, rather then fully listening, you are thinking about your next response. By doing these two things at the same time, not only will you miss some of what is being said, but you will also not take the time to process what is being said.

For example: Husband comes home after a long day at work.

Wife says: "You know I really hate it when you take off your shoes and tie and leave them in the living room."

Husband responds, "Well I wouldn't do that if the house already wasn't so messy. I thought it really didn't matter."

The problem with this interaction is that neither person is really listening to what the other person is saying. The dialogue simply becomes a pet peeve ping-pong match.

Consider the alternative.

Wife says "You know I really hate it when you leave your shoes and tie in the living room,"

Husband says, "You know, I have some issues with some of your habits, but I'll tell you what: I'm willing to hear and address your issues today, if we can agree to talk about my issues tomorrow."

Wife at that point will probably say, "OK".

The conversation from that point on may be very short and may be limited to the simple fact that wife hates when husband's shoes and ties are not put away. It may even result in a continuing conversation that wife is under stress and it's not really about the shoes and ties.

If the husband and wife can simply agree to listen and focus exclusively on the other person's concerns and issues, the dynamic has completely changed. Wife feels heard and husband realizes it's really not about the shoes at all. True communication has begun. Instead of engaging in the ping-pong match, the couple is now engaged in listening and cooperating to find real solutions. The simple act of agreeing that one person will have the floor and that both will focus on his or her issue completely, and the other person will get a chance later on, is the single, most dramatic and effective technique there is to help people listen and resolve their differences. Other techniques, including reframing, rephrasing, and acknowledging, are also important. But just listening is the easiest and most effective.

CHAPTER 11
PREMARITAL AGREEMENTS

So far, we've discussed the bumpy road to divorce. Sometimes, an ounce of prevention is worth a pound of cure. And in this area of life the ounce is a premarital agreement.

Ah... the dreaded prenup. Often necessary, seldom appreciated and sometimes more difficult to negotiate as a lawyer than a mediated dissolution. I guess it's because in divorce there really aren't a lot of expectations of having everything work out perfectly and amicably, because the parties are no longer in love and so, not necessarily motivated to be nice and make compromises.

With a prenup, however, the parties are often still in the honeymoon phase of the relationship and so talking about its demise all seems a bit surreal.

While the law governing marriage in California is designed to be fair and protect a husband and wife, sometimes in its application, an opposite result occurs.

The law treats marriage as a contract with a myriad of terms and conditions that take effect once the "I do's" have been said. The benefits of having a premarital agreement is that rather than the state of California determining the terms that will govern your marriage, you and your spouse get to do so. So, while you are still in love and want to be fair to each other and work out an agreement that both of you can live with, you can do so by preparing a premarital agreement. The other option is to go blindly into wedded bliss and then, if it doesn't work out, perhaps be the deer in the headlights knocking on a divorce attorney's door.

Actually, my initial goal in meeting with a client who is interested in drafting a prenup is to see if it can be avoided in the first place. It's important to determine a client's objectives and then discuss them in light of California law - and in this case a little knowledge can be all they need. Depending on what one's assets are, and what he/she is trying to achieve, there are times that with the proper planning, a premarital agreement can be avoided altogether. In cases where this isn't possible i.e. there is no way to keep a business interest separate without one, all I can say is, it's probably best to write one up - and expect some tears.

THE LIGHTER SIDE OF DIVORCE

He taught me housekeeping. When I divorce, I keep the house.

Zsa Zsa Gabor

If you think you had trouble supporting a wife.... try not supporting her.

Anonymous

It takes two to destroy a marriage.

Margaret Trudeaux

My divorce came to me as a complete surprise. That's what happens when you haven't been home in 18 years.

Lee Travino

You never really know a man until you've divorced him.

Zsa Zsa Gabor

Why do Jewish divorces cost so much? They're worth it.

Henny Youngman

I never married, but I tell people I'm divorced so they won't think there's something wrong with me.

Elayne Boosler

BOOK TWO – DEATH

INTRODUCTION

When David found out he was going to inherit a fortune once his sickly father died, he decided he needed a woman to enjoy it with. So one evening, he went to a singles bar where he spotted the most beautiful woman he had ever seen. Her natural beauty took his breath away.

"I may look like just an ordinary man, " he said as he approached her, "but in just a few years, my father will die and I'll inherit 20 million dollars."

Impressed, the woman went home with him that evening and, a week later, she became his stepmother.

Women are so much better at estate planning then men.

Actually, in my experience the genders approach estate planning with about the same enthusiasm. That being said, it does seem that in many cases it is the wife that makes the first call, makes the first appointment, and gathers the necessary information I will need to make my recommendations and prepare the documents. For whatever reason, it seems that women are more willing to address their own mortality than men. In any event, whether it's the wife dragging in the husband or the husband dragging in the wife, just get yourself to an attorney and plan your estate. It's really amazing how just a little bit of planning can make a huge difference.

I give talks to small groups of moms (and a few dads) at my local "mommy and me" preschool and it always amazes me how many parents do not have any estate plan in place. In a group of 20, the average show of hands for those who have a trust or will is usually about two or three. By the end of the hour, after I tell them all the wonderful options they have for estate planning after their demise, and all of the horrible consequences if they do nothing and opt for California's make shift plan, for the most part, I leave a room full of anxious parents promising themselves to make estate planning a priority.

Sure, the odds that you young whippersnappers will die an early, sudden and unexpected death without an estate plan in place are somewhat slim, but why take that risk if you don't have to? People will go beyond their means to make certain their children are their number one priority and receive the best of everything they have to offer, except when it comes to easing the heirs' burden should they die unexpectedly. Actually, even clients who know their time on this planet is limited will often wait until the bitter end. I can't tell you the number of times I've spent in hospitals, often only to tell the family members it's too late, because their loved one no longer has the capacity to sign any documents.

I guess because the reward in taking the time and spending the money to do an estate plan is such an intangible one, it's set on the back burner of the ever increasing to-do list that all of us have. All I can offer here is to say that for my clients who do finally bite the bullet and get a plan, the relief on their faces when they leave my office after our signing meeting is palpable.

One last tidbit that doesn't, in my opinion, deserve an entire chapter, but which I do think is important enough to mention, is life insurance. I'm not a big proponent of the stuff, except in the case where you have young children and a relatively small estate. A 20-year term policy of $1,000,000 for a younger couple is pretty inexpensive. Especially when considering the fact that as you get older or start to have health issues, the prices can go up considerably. If you get life insurance while the kids are young, 20 years is really all you need to make sure that if something does happen to you during that time, your children will have the money they need to continue to lead a comfortable life until they are old enough to start making enough to pay for their needs on their own.

When is that by the way? As a mother of a small herd of daughters just out of college, I ask myself that question a lot. In any event, it can be a great benefit to have a policy in place. Not only will it help your children, but it will also help relieve the financial burden of the guardian you've selected who is responsible for raising them after you are gone.

So, I'm assuming, if you are reading this book, you are one of those people who have put off estate planning. You are still thinking that you might at some point, maybe in the not so distant future, if you get a little extra time, and money, and the planets all align in just the right configuration – THEN, you will get a plan in place. But in the meantime you want to learn a little more about it. That being said, you may also be one of those people who went to a lawyer awhile back, got an estate plan, and are just looking to refresh your memory about what you did and why. Whatever your purpose for reading these pages, my goal is to inform and educate, and get those rusty wheels turning so that you can hop into the driver's seat and finally get a plan in place. You will hopefully be able to discern from the chapter titles whether the information that follows is relevant and worth your time to read. Most of the information will be relevant to the majority of you and worth the read in its entirety, except perhaps the passages on guardians of young children. In the event that your children are all grown up (do they ever grow up?), some of the issues you needed to plan for when they were young no longer exist.

CHAPTER 1

YOU THOUGHT DEATH WAS SCARY? FACING PROBATE CAN BE DOWNRIGHT FRIGHTENING

Dealing with the difficult emotional aspects of death is just the tip of the iceberg, compared to the financial difficulties that can soon ensue - especially when the deceased had either no estate plan or an inadequate one.

Fees associated with Probate, which is the procedure whereby the court oversees the administration of a will, are statutory, at least in California. They are set in the probate code as a percentage of the size of the estate and are based on the *gross* value of the estate, not the net. So you could own a house that's worth $1,000,000 that has a $900,000 mortgage and guess what? The probate fees are based on the entire $1,000,000, which currently will cost you fees of $46,000! Hardly seems fair I know. What's really unfair is that I, the lawyer, now have to explain to the grieving widow that she has to sell her only asset (the house) in order to pay the probate fees!

Fortunately, between a husband and wife, there are sometimes summary proceedings so a full probate, and the associated fees, typically aren't necessary. In that case, rather than a set fee, attorneys typically will charge an hourly rate... uh oh. Many attorneys however will still charge a fixed fee based on the size of the estate and relate it back to the statutory probate fees... again, uh oh. Almost always, the better option is to prepare a living trust, which avoids court involvement altogether, be it a probate or other summary proceeding.

By the way, if you think you are smarter than the average bear and will avoid probate by giving away the house to your adoring children while you are still alive, be warned, Yogi Bear.

Let's assume your child really is a saint, and you decide to deed your house to her while you are alive. It seems so much easier and cheaper than the whole will/

trust thing, right? Right! You think you can save a bundle on legal fees, not only in preparing the estate plan, but also in handling its administration after you die because the child already owns the house. Seems too good to be true?

Well, first lets address the obvious. Yes, your daughter is a saint, but who could have predicted the car accident she would have with the mean man, whose shyster attorney is now suing her for everything she owns - including your house. Or, how about when saintly daughter marries evil son-in-law, who convinces her that they should go ahead and live in the house now and you would be much better in that lovely retirement home in the next county. Or, how about when saintly daughter becomes incapacitated, probably driven crazy by evil son-in-law, and now neither she, nor you by proxy, has any control over what happens to the house.

I know, all of these scenarios seem pretty unlikely, but butter my buns and call me a biscuit, stuff like this happens more often than one would think. Money does loony stuff to people.

So, lets assume that everything has been hunky dory and aging mom put daughter on the title to her home. Daughter married Dudley Doright. Daughter had no credit problems or bad financial luck of her own. She let mom continue to live in the house until mom died. So now it all turned out OK, right?

Wrong. Because you see, there's this pesky rule in the tax laws that makes this kind of makeshift estate planning a disaster. It goes something like this: Let's say you bought your house many, many, many years ago in Manhattan Beach, California, for $100,000. (Ah, the good old days.... if only I knew then what I know now....).

That $100,000 is called your cost basis. Now, you sell your tiny little house for $1,500,000 lot value. God Bless America. You will have to pay capital gains tax on the profit, which is $1,400,000. Yikes. Of course you may be entitled to an exclusion, currently $250,000, so you only have taxes on $1,150,000. Still, yikes.

However, if you keep the house until you die, the beneficiaries who inherit it upon your death (whether by will or trust), will do so with an increase in the cost basis to the value at your date of death.

So in this case, let's say you left the house to your niece, and at your death it had a fair market value of $1,500.000, that would be the cost basis for your niece. So if she decides to sell it right away and does so for $1,500,000, there is no profit or gain so therefore, no capital gains taxes. However, if you had given it to her before you died, she would take your cost basis, i.e. $100,000, and for the same sale, she would have capital gain of $1,400,000!

This is true for any gifts given during life; the recipient of the gift keeps the same cost basis that the giver had. So, at least for highly appreciated property, for income tax reasons, it's generally not a good idea to make the gift while you are still alive.

Another possible way to avoid probate is to have a beneficiary designated on all of your assets in the event of your death. More and more institutions allow this for including bank and brokerage accounts. Historically, you could not name a beneficiary for real property (i.e. your home), however more and more states are beginning to recognize TOD -Transfer on Death - deeds.

Unfortunately California, as of yet, is not one of them. It seems the State Bar has some very powerful lobbyists who continually shut down any legislative attempts to allow this. Their arguments are that it would be too easy to abuse and fraudulent TOD deeds would flood the system. Hmmm.

That's their same argument for justifying California's probate process, which is one of the most intricate, rule laden, time consuming, and expensive systems of all the states.

Some states (California is not one of them) even have an "opt out" clause in the law that will allow beneficiaries of a will to forgo a full probate in the case where all the beneficiaries and the executor agree that they don't want, or need, the protection or oversight of the court. It seems that for California it may be less about keeping a lot of complicated safeguards in place as it is about having to hire attorneys, because they are the only ones who know how to maneuver through the court and the quagmire of rules in place!

CHAPTER 2

NO PLAN? GUESS WHAT, THE STATE WILL CREATE ONE FOR YOU!

If, like many people out there, you are dead set against planning for your death, be warned, the law has its own set of rules to fill the gap. When you do not have any kind of plan in place, i.e. a will, living trust, or the like, the state of California will fall back on their "intestate laws" to determine who will be the lucky winners of your accumulated wealth. Each state has its own intestate laws but most are somewhat similar to those of California.

The thinking behind the rules is that if someone dies without a will, who would they, typically, want to inherit their assets? The problem of course is that the state's assumptions about who should inherit will not always lead to optimal results, and sometimes can result in disaster.

For example, if you have children, the law assumes that most people without a will would want their children to be the beneficiaries of their estate. If you die without a will in California and you have no spouse, but leave surviving children, they will split your assets equally. Sounds good?

Possibly.

However, what if you have a spouse and children? In that case, your community property (the assets you have accumulated during the marriage) will all go to your spouse and your separate property (the property you had before marriage or were gifted/inherited during marriage) will be shared between your spouse and children. (The distinction between community and separate property in California is a bit more complicated than that.) Still sounds good?

What if you have accumulated a nice size estate over the years and have many adoring children. Divorced for many years and just about ready to give up on love, you meet the man of your dreams on a seniors cruise to Alaska and fall madly in love. You get married soon after... ah... impetuous youth.

Not much later, you catch Mr. Right stealing jewelry from your secret hiding place and the shock causes you to keel over with a massive heart attack and die. Now what? Well, even though you were married a short time, Mr. Right (more like Mr. Right Now) will inherit *all* your community property. Granted there probably won't be a lot of it since you haven't been married long. But he will also inherit one-half of your separate property! Your poor kids may spend the next 10 years of their lives in court trying to change this outcome, but the odds of winning are stacked against them – because the law is stacked against them.

CHAPTER 3

WE DO IT FOR THE KIDS: PROTECTING YOUR CHILDREN'S INHERITANCE

Before I get into the nitty gritty of the different options there are for leaving your assets to your children, I'd like to address the "I Know this Sounds Horrible but I Want You to Take My Son (daughter, dog, whatever applies) Out of My Will" syndrome.

Actually, as an estate planning attorney, and a mother of four delightful daughters myself, I get this a lot less frequently than I imagined. But I do get it occasionally.

The first time I had only been practicing for a few years. I immediately drafted an amendment to my clients living trust and they came in to sign a few days later. Six months later we were doing another amendment to add back the recalcitrant heir.

My point is that before you call your attorney to disinherit a loved one, sleep on it. Kids grow up and realize you are not the enemy. Kids get over their stint of experimenting with drugs. Kids fall out of love with the leader of a wayward cult. Kids decide maybe they do want to get a job and contribute to society. Kids start taking their medication. Whatever it is: give it some time. And if the infraction they participated in doesn't go away, you may nevertheless decide you still want them in your will. Time has a way of lessening the initial sting of a loved one doing you wrong. And if you take your kids out of your will and die before you had a chance to forgive them, you will forever leave this planet with that exit. Is that really how you want to be remembered? Maybe.

So, assuming you have forgiven your children and you do want to leave them your estate after all, what's the best way to do so?

Your two basic options are to leave them everything outright, or put everything in a trust for their benefit. The reason for doing the latter is typically because they are not mature enough to handle a huge inheritance responsibly. I know, I know - are they ever?

In a children's trust, you direct the person in charge, the Trustee, to distribute money from the trust to your children while they are growing up, typically for their health, support and education. Then, at some age you specify, they get the balance outright and the trust terminates. The magical age for many of my clients is somewhere around 25 or 30 or perhaps in stages, so they would receive one-half at 25, and the balance at 30. While the money is held in trust, not only is it protected from the child spending it irresponsibly, it's also protected from the child's creditors, as well as their spouses should they later divorce.

I remember when my daughters turned 18; they were inundated with credit card offers. Of course, I took them to the office and shredded them before they even knew. But unless you can shred from the grave, and your children do take up these companies on their wonderful offers to buy cash at a mere 27% interest - it could get ugly quickly. However, if they don't get the money outright until they are 30, hopefully by then they will have learned a thing or two about finances and will still have something left to invest!

But what about the dreaded and evil son-in-law? Let's say your now rich 19-year old daughter ends up marrying her high school sweetheart, or any one of the handsome suitors that come out of the woodwork professing their love for her, once they hear about her new found loot. What happens when the marriage doesn't work out?

Community property laws in California, and in many other states as well, sometimes fly in the face of what may seem fair. It's actually pretty easy to commingle an inheritance, which starts out as separate property, in such a way that upon divorce, a big chunk of it is up for grabs. Now she's divorced, poor, and raising two kids on her own.

If you can keep the money in trust, then it can't be commingled, and will be protected from divorce proceedings. The thinking here is that by the time she turns 30 and has full access to the money, she will make a better choice for a spouse, and better yet, become educated on how to keep the inheritance separate, and even better still, get a prenup! From your lips to God's ears - ah, one can only hope.

One last word of warning: in case of your early demise such that your children inherit your estate while they are still very young. If you don't set up a trust for them, getting a boatload of cash at a young age is just the tip of the iceberg. Because now, the court must get involved to oversee the administration of the young heirs' inheritance.

The law will not let children under 18 inherit anything outright. Rather, they will appoint someone to manage the child's money - the guardian of the estate - until he or she turns 18, at which point the guardianship ends and the balance is distributed.

The courts, in an effort to protect the inheritance, monitor the guardianship very closely. While this sounds good in theory, in practice it's a bad, bad thing that's getting worse every day. Because every year, the guardian must hire an attorney, ugh, and put together a long and involved report and an accounting about the guardian's actions during that period. After they submit the report, then they must go to court and justify it all.

Even in the good old days, when there were lots of courts that were fully staffed, this was a long, painful and expensive process. Now, with all of the district probate court closures and the overloaded and understaffed probate court downtown, the process has become unbearable.

As I wind up my remaining guardianships, I, like many of my colleagues, have vowed not to accept any new cases. You just can't pay us enough - shocking, I know! I guess even attorneys have a price!!!

And the kicker is, that all the protection offered by the court's overseeing the guardian's acts is available to the children even if they had inherited the assets in a trust - without any court involvement at all.

In a children's trust, the trustee is required to report and account to the children directly - or the adult taking care of them. So there is the same protection and oversight. Typically, the trustee, the child, and the child's caregiver - guardian of the person - can present informal accountings with all the necessary information and without court involvement and attorney time. But if something is amiss, and the trustee has breached a duty, then he or she can be made to answer to the court at that point.

CHAPTER 4

THE AB TRUST: SAVE ESTATE TAXES AND PROTECT YOUR SPOUSE FROM CHANGING YOUR BENEFICIARIES AFTER YOU DIE

Remember the old saying about the two things you can't avoid, death and taxes? Well actually, there are three things you can't avoid, Death, Taxes, and Death Taxes! Really!? OK, now run to your window, open it up and shout, "I'm mad as hell and I'm not going to take it anymore" (for you older movie fans. "Network" circa 1976).

Fortunately, once your heirs add up the value of all of your assets to determine your estate tax, also known appropriately as the death tax, the Federal government allows a credit against every estate and the taxable estate is only everything over this credit amount. The really good news is that recently this credit amount was raised to $5,000,000 per person (indexed for inflation so that currently in 2014 the amount is up to $5,340,000). Woo Whoo! Not too long ago the credit was a mere million which meant that even an average person who happened to own a home in California that they bought way back when there was still affordable housing out here, often had to pay the government a whopping tax at death - around 50%!

In order to help alleviate the estate tax problem, which at that time affected lots of people, the legal community got together and devised complicated estate plans and trusts with the goal of minimizing these taxes. Today, with the credit amount at $5,340,000 per person or, thanks to the new "Portability" law, $10,680,000 for a married couple, only the very wealthy are potentially faced with estate taxes at their death, so these complicated plans are no longer necessary for the average Joe.

That being said, there's an element in one of the most popular plans - I call it an AB or an ABC living trust - that still has other non-tax benefits that some of my clients find attractive.

Imagine the following: William and Kate married for 10 years with two lovely young children, Phil and Charlie. Then one day, wham, William is in a horrible polo accident, is thrown from his horse, hits a tree head-on and dies instantly. Fortunately, he had a sizeable estate and a living trust in place that leaves everything to Kate. Kate mourns him for the appropriate amount of time, and then decides to move on and ends up marrying Harry - a bit of a pauper but cute as a button.

Well, then fertile Kate ends up having four more children with Harry. They live a long and happy life, but Kate eventually kicks the bucket. (Yet another euphemism for death, rumored to be from hanging oneself by "kicking the bucket" out from underneath.) So Kate dies and her estate plan leaves everything to Harry. Harry, never really fond of William's children, dies soon after, and leaves his estate, which is still mostly comprised of assets that came from William, to his own four children. Poor Charlie and Phil! Yes, indeed. Without mum around to fund the life style they had grown accustomed to, and without any inheritance whatsoever, *poor* Charlie and Phil.

Or what about this twist on our scenario: Imagine Kate mourned William's death for most of her life. Finally, in her late eighties, she meets a nice younger man, John, and decides to tie the knot rather than die alone. They have an elaborate wedding. She still has quite a sizable estate thanks to William. She is run down a couple days later on the sidewalk outside her attorney's office by a hit and run driver. She was meeting with the attorney to finally make a will in which she was leaving everything to her children.

Shame. And double shame because without a will or trust, the intestate laws apply as discussed more fully in chapter 2, and a huge chunk of her assets go to some John.

So, you see, whether from bad intentions or just simple neglect, if you are married and are the first spouse to die leaving everything to the surviving spouse, you really have no idea if, at their death, they will have left your share of the estate to your children. This is especially true where there are stepchildren thrown in the mix. If you have children from a former marriage, can you be certain that if you die first leaving everything to your current wife, that she will carry out your wishes and leave what's left at her death to your children, her stepchildren? Especially if she has children of her own, to whom she may want to leave everything.

The solution? The AB Trust! Finally a way to control your estate *from your grave!* Thanks be to God!! Essentially what it does is split your family trust into two trusts when the first spouse dies. One trust, the B trust, consists of the assets of the deceased spouse, the first spouse to die. The A trust contains the survivor's assets. The surviving spouse has access to the B trust for her needs while she is still alive - you can choose how much access to give her - but when she dies, whatever is remaining in the B trust will go to the remaining beneficiaries you initially set up and she can't change this.

Because of the limitations of the B trust and other factors, such as having to answer to the remaining beneficiaries while the surviving spouse is still living - awkward - it's important to have a thorough understanding of the all the benefits and disadvantages of this type of trust before deciding to onset one up. A good estate-planning attorney will take the time to explain it to you fully and answer any questions you have, so your decision to create it will be an informed one.

CHAPTER 5

LET'S SPEND $30,000 FIGHTING OVER A $30 TOASTER

Interestingly enough, some of the worst lawsuits in terms of length, escalating attorneys fees, and refusal to settle, aren't about money at all. Rather, they are based on principle, hurt feelings, and miscommunication.

One example that comes to mind is a case I heard in a Los Angeles probate court. I was waiting for the judge to call my case, and I had the pleasure of listening to some forty or more before mine.

Before I launch in, let me expound, if I may. Court is actually quite interesting if you have the gumption and spare time. If you ever want to get a taste of what you, or your loved ones - whoever is left behind to sort out the legal mess after a death - will face in court when there is no plan in place, go sit in your neighborhood court for a day.

Due to budget constraints and cut backs, the Los Angeles County Superior Court now holds all of its probate proceedings in the downtown Los Angeles courthouse. In the good old days, one could file their probate in a district court, where the decedent resided. Many of my cases were often handled at the Torrance courthouse. Without going into a lot of boring detail regarding the ramifications of cutbacks, suffice to say, that as the number of probate proceedings continues to rise, the number of courts, judges and court staff continues to decline. Thus, the procedure for moving even a simple case through the system is becoming almost impossible. Trust me, you don't want to be in court if you don't have to - and with proper planning you typically don't have to.

So, anyway, one of the cases before mine on this particular day was a family of four siblings whose mother had passed away. She had no living trust, clearly, or they probably would not have been in court in the first place. And no will either. Apparently, there were a couple of personal items that she, along the way, had promised to more than one child. They were all in court arguing about which of the four should be in charge of the probate because none of them trusted the other and because they had all shown up at mom's house at various times after she died and taken things from her home.

The two who had filed the initial petition and were appointed as co-executors wanted to remain as such. And the other two wanted to replace them and serve in their place. They each had a lawyer present who was equally interested in the outcome, because if their client won, the lawyer would come in as a package deal. The judge intimated on several occasions that it was a fairly modest estate and the ensuing battle hardly seemed worth it. To top things off, the prized possession, that would eventually be fought over at another future hearing, was an old, monetarily worthless painting that mom had retired to the basement years before.

Fortunately, the judge, who was a gentleman with whom I happened to attend law school, had the wisdom to recommend that none of them serve as executor. This would help nip in the bud not only the current fight, but also all the fights likely to come later on in probate. He "strongly suggested" they agree to appoint a private fiduciary to serve as the executor. Last I saw, he had sent them all out into the hallway to discuss this option.

So, take note potential planners, it's oftentimes the personal effects with little or no value that can cause the biggest fights among the surviving family members. What you may think is a silly little trinket not worth mentioning may be the difference between an uneventful and relatively smooth estate administration, and an all out family feud. Search your memory banks, or even ask your children, to see if there's something of sentimental worth they would like you to leave to them as part of your trust.

Another option, especially if you are older, is to start giving away stuff you are willing to part with while you are still alive. Not only do you eliminate the potential "I'm certain mom wanted me to have it," but also you get to experience the joy of giving the gift, which is half the fun anyway! And, of course, if you can't part with it while you are alive, and you can't choose who of your marvelous offspring should get what, there are other ways to handle it in your will or trust. A good estate-planning attorney can give guidance here.

CHAPTER 6

NO ONE CAN LOVE MY KIDS LIKE I DO: PICKING A GUARDIAN TO RAISE YOUR BUNDLES OF JOY

While it may be true that no one can love a child in the way that a parent can, when it comes to picking a guardian for the little rug rats, keep in mind it's still better that you pick the best of the bad, rather than leave it up to the court to appoint someone after you are gone. In fact, clients often tell me that choosing a guardian to raise their children is the most difficult decision they face. So much so, that they put the entire estate planning process on hold because of it. Either mom and dad can't agree on the same person, or they both agree that there is no one out there who is worthy of the "privilege." Or, as parents of teenage girls often say, the "sentence" of raising the little darlings.

Possibly the best tip I can give my clients is to plan as if your death was "now." If mom and dad both kicked the bucket today, who would be the best choice to raise the children? Because, keep in mind that life happens, people and situations change, and what may be a good idea now, could be a not-so-good idea down the road.

In my practice, the guardian is the most commonly changed aspect of an estate plan.

For example, you may pick someone who ends up marrying someone you hate. You may pick someone who is married to someone you love, and they end up getting a divorce. You may pick someone local who moves somewhere that you think is too far away. You may pick someone with no kids, who then has a bunch of their own later on. You may settle on someone, and then meet the perfect person later on. You may pick one of your parents who becomes too old down the road.

People change, life happens. Look at your current situation, and be guided by what would be in the best interest of your child. That's what the court is guided by when they have to pick. And more important, be ready to readdress it occasionally, or quite often, if you have a lot of changes in your life, to see if the person(s) you've selected is/are still the best choice.

Another thing to keep in mind is to talk to the person you are thinking of choosing to make sure he/she is up for the task. Believe it or not, some may say that although they love your kids dearly, they do not want to parent them. Do not take this personally. You've arguably already put them in a rather delicate and difficult position by asking. It's better to know that they won't do it, than to name them and then have them decline later on.

That being said, some family dynamics may warrant a different course of action.

For example, if you have three sisters you love the same, and are trying to choose between them, once you do decide, it might be best to keep it to yourself. By telling them whom you have chosen, and whom you have de-facto rejected, you run the risk of hurting their feelings and causing family disharmony for something that will likely never occur. Odds are, one or both parents will outlive the child's 18th birthday, so no one will ever need to know whom you picked. Of course that doesn't mean you still shouldn't do your Will and name your guardian. The peace of mind for having done so will far outweigh the odds that it will ever come to be. My best advice here is to look at your family situation and do what makes the most sense in your case.

Other things to keep in mind:

1. If you select someone and they serve for a while and then they can't serve anymore for whatever reason,

your children are not going to end up with their choice for a guardian. Rather, the court will go back to your next choice. So if you are thinking of making your wonderful best friend Grace the guardian, but you are afraid that ultimately the kids may end up with Grace's crazy aunt Matilda whom she adores, your children will not end up with Aunt Matilda. That is unless you perhaps have not named an alternate, and no one else comes forward to serve. Funny we use the term "serve" as a guardian – like it's a prison sentence.

2. If you want your brother to serve and he is married, then you have to decide if you want just him - or him and his wife - as co-guardians. There's no right answer here. It all depends on whether you want both of them to have all the rights and powers that being guardian entails – such as making decisions for health, education, religion etc. If you do want to make them co-guardians, then you should specify what happens in the case of death. Should they stay with the survivor, or go to your plan b choice?

Or, if there's a divorce, which parent should now be the sole guardian?

I actually had a case where mom and dad had chosen mom's brother and his wife to be co-guardians and if they divorced while serving as guardians, the children were to stay with the wife! This brings me to a point that should be clear, but just in case there's any confusion: you cannot pick co-guardians that are not married. Of course, you could try to do so in the guardian nomination in your Will, but the odds that the Court would allow it are slim to none.

Except in the movies! Remember "Life As We Know It" with Katherine Heigl and Josh Duhamel? Two complete strangers are named to co-parent a friend's child? It may have actually been a cute movie concept, but I was so caught up in the legalities of the impossibility of the plot, that I couldn't really enjoy it.

CHAPTER 7

NO ONE CAN LOVE MY MONEY LIKE I DO: PICKING THE LUCKY SOUL IN CHARGE OF YOUR CHILDREN'S MONEY

Having decided who will raise your little miracles from God, you can now let out a heavy sigh of relief that at least *that* decision is over and it's all smooth sailing ahead.

Uh oh, tsunami on the horizon! Or maybe just a few waves. Because now you must decide who will be in charge of all the massive wealth you will leave to your young progeny. Should it be the same person who you've named as guardian to raise them? Assuming you were listening above and have opted for a children's trust, rather than the default - a guardian of the estate - the person who handles any money you've left to the kids is called the trustee.

So, should your brother Sue (for you Johnny Cash fans), who has so graciously agreed to raise your children, also be the trustee? In a perfect world, yes. It's certainly the easiest course to take. He is raising them, so he knows their needs and has easy access to the money.

But hold on, cowboy.

Is this really the best course of action? Remember how money does horrible things to people in the worst-case scenario, and skews their judgment in the best-case scenario? Money just has a tendency to blur the lines of yours, mine and ours for even the best intentioned.

Take Sue for example. Now that he has three more kids to raise, he decides he needs a bigger house. Okey dokey, so far.

So he meditates on it, and decides that rather then add an addition to his home, he should buy that new house down the street - the three story one with the private listing and plantation shutters that just came on the market. And, of course, he will use the children's money because they are the reason he needs the bigger house and anyways, they will get to live there.

All of this *might* be copasetic if he put their name - actually the trust name - on the title. But Sue didn't know this and didn't want to spend money on a lawyer to find out.

Or maybe Sue sees the evil of his ways, and forgoes the new house. But what about the car? His Prius will not fit his growing brood, so he trades it in for the top of the line Range Rover with the great safety ratings. Sweet. A Chevy cargo van probably would've worked fine. Just throw them all in the back, like our parents did with us! But hey, not a big deal.

Now if someone else – let's call him Bob - was the trustee and Sue wanted to buy the new three story house with the private listing and plantation shutters, he would have to get Bob's approval and you can bet our story would have a different ending.

And what about the case where our business savvy 14 year old ward who asks uncle Sue for an accounting of the year's trust transactions and discovers that well-meaning Sue lost a bunch in the stock market? Sue of course justifies his actions by saying everyone who was anyone thought the stock was solid and a great investment. So now what?

Does little Johnny sue Sue?

Johnny may very well have a cause of action if Sue was negligent. But should he be suing the same person who is raising him? Talk about a strained relationship. And if not, what about the shrunken inheritance? Should Johnny just forgive and forget?

Just saying – this is a problem that could easily have been skirted if the trustee and the guardian were not the same person.

And finally, let's assume that everything is going swimmingly.

Sue has invested wisely and made the trust a lot of money, or at least kept the principal intact. Nor has he crossed any gray lines by benefitting himself with the trust money.

Now, little Johnny, all grown up into big John, is turning 16 and wants a big shindig of a birthday party. Fair enough. He is also keen on the fact that mom and dad - may they rest in peace - had a huge term-life insurance policy in place when they died, and there is over one million dollars in a trust for his benefit.

So he asks his replacement dad Uncle Sue (I know, no one can replace you!) who is also the trustee, if he can have a Ferrari for his birthday. Of course he has totally justified it in his own little 16-year old brain, given that he has over a million dollars that he will eventually get - hopefully not until he's 30 - and there's so much money and after all it's *his* money.

But Uncle Sue says "No!" Probably. Hopefully.

Now all Johnny can think about is how dad would have given him the Ferrari and how much he hates mean Uncle Sue. Remember, 16-year-old brain here. And in my scenario the child is male. Can you imagine the same story with a pubescent teenage girl who wants a pony??? I shudder to think.

In this scenario, if the trustee was someone other than Uncle Sue, he could merely tell Johnny to "Go ask the trustee. She is in charge of the money." Done.

CHAPTER 8

FREE FORMS: THE GOOD, THE BAD, AND THE UGLY

In case you're wondering if you can just scratch something out on paper that would count as a Will:

If you live in California you *can* write your own Will, and if it satisfies the legal requirements for a valid Will, the court doesn't care if it's scribbled on the back of a napkin! It's called a Holographic Will and must be entirely in your own handwriting, signed and dated. Unlike a typed Will, the usual mandatory two witnesses are not required, nor does it need to be notarized. There are still other requirements for a valid Will, i.e. it must show testamentary intent, so before you go running to your desk to grab a piece of paper and pencil, please read on.

Whether you don't have the time to see a lawyer, or if you feel you just can't afford one right now, there is another option you can choose, UNTIL YOU CAN SEE A LAWYER AND GET IT DONE PROPERLY. What I don't recommend is that you purchase one of the many "do it yourself" software packages available. I've seen some of the documents they produce, and they scare me. In most cases, I think you are better off with no plan than a bad plan. Remember, the state creates a will for you if you die without one. Better to rely on the wisdom of the state than a company not necessarily familiar with California law and really only in it to make a buck.

The best Plan B in my opinion is to use the Statutory Will form provided by the state of California. Not only is it free, it comes with a wealth of information about how to fill it out as well as what it does and doesn't do and it covers all the areas a good Will should. Basically, all you have to do is fill in the blanks. It allows you to waive the bond otherwise required by the courts during a probate, which can save your heirs a lot of money. A bond to cover any monetary losses incurred by a negligent or malicious executor can be helpful, but if you trust your executor and he does his job well, then paying a fee to have him bonded can be a waste of money.

The California statutory will also allows you to appoint a custodian to be in charge of any money your minor child inherits, up until the child turns 25. Though not as flexible as a child's trust that you would create as part of a living trust, it does avoid a court ordered guardianship of the estate, and it also has the benefit of delaying outright distribution to the children until they are 25 (rather then the default age of 18).

My personal experience is that the difference in the level of responsibility in my daughters from the age of 18 to 25 is vast and if I could prolong an outright distribution to them until they are 25 that would be good. Remember the California Statutory Will, or any Will for that matter, DOES NOT AVOID PROBATE! The best way to avoid a probate is with a Living Trust and there is no California Trust form.

Another document you should have in your arsenal of free forms is the Power of Attorney for Property. A power of attorney appoints a person to act as your agent should you become incapacitated. It gives that person the ability to access your bank accounts, pay your bills, and typically sign any legal documents that need to be signed during your incapacity. It is an important component to an estate plan and avoids a conservatorship, which is what you would have to otherwise face. A conservatorship is a court-ordered procedure, which appoints an agent (conservator) to be in charge of your finances if you are incapacitated and unable to do it on your own.

For a married couple, the conservator appointed will typically be the person's spouse. The legal fees in setting up the conservatorship in addition to the required subsequent annual court hearings to monitor it can be quite high, not to mention the time required and emotional stress. The California statutory power of attorney is thorough and allows you to select exactly which powers you would like your agent to have. Banks aren't keen on honoring powers of attorney, but after some convincing, they eventually do. They fear liability if the agent screws up, but probably more likely they fear once the agent takes control of the account, they will move the funds to their own bank as a matter of convenience.

In any event, although an attorney drafted power of attorney can be tailored to the needs of the client, the banks get a warm fuzzy feeling with a California form and so may be even more likely to honor it. In fact, oftentimes, banks and other various financial institutions will have their own Powers of Attorney. Just ask. Of course, the benefit here, if the bank has drafted its own Power of Attorney, it will be even more likely to accept it – you would think. In any event, the California forms may vary in appearance, but are all drafted pursuant to the laws regarding California Uniform Statutory Form Power of Attorney and can be found free of charge at various resources online.

Advance Health Care Directive. Argg. How many of you remember the Terry Schiavo fiasco back in 2005? In 1990 she collapsed for an unknown reason and soon after was diagnosed as being in a "persistent vegetative state". What then followed was a long court battle between her husband who, after years of unsuccessful attempts to bring her back, wanted to remove life support, and her parents who wanted to keep her alive at all costs, and I mean *all costs.*

Because she had not prepared a health care directive stating her wishes or appointing an agent, the court battle lingered. It wasn't until 2005 that the courts finally agreed with her husband, and she was allowed to die. Interestingly enough, after the case was over a poll was taken of doctors in the AMA (American Medical Association). 62% of them said that they would also send it to court to let a judge decide. And this was true even if everything *was* in place i.e. a valid power of attorney with an agent asking to remove life support and the doctor's concurrence.

So the biggest lesson here, in addition to preparing a valid health care directive, is to talk with your family members and friends. Tell them your thoughts and wishes so its less likely one of them will intervene. Note also that California law has a provision that allows "any interested person or friend" to petition the court and challenge a health care agent's actions regardless whether the agent is acting under a valid health care directive! The law goes on to say that you can eliminate this possibility if you have an attorney drafted health care directive that does so. Hence, even though you can use a form prepared pursuant to California law, you will not have this very important option to make sure you do not end up in a hospital in a vegetative state for many years while some "interested person" and the courts decide your fate.

So there it is. Although not as good as an attorney drafted estate plan that is tailored to your specific needs and can avoid probate, these three forms I've discussed above are certainly better than nothing, and they are free! OK? So now get up and go get your laptop and a pen and have at it! No excuses!

THE LIGHTER SIDE OF DEATH

For those of you who just want to cut to the chase and not bother with all the boring details and explanations I have set forth in the book, I offer the following:

Top Ten Reasons for Having a Good Estate Plan in Place Before You Die.

Reason number ten:

It can save your heirs a boatload of money in probate fees.

Reason number nine:

It can save your heirs a boatload of time in the administration of your estate.

Reason number eight:

It can save your estate a boatload of money in death taxes.

Reason number seven:

If you go crazy, it can prevent a court ordered conservatorship (saving you a boatload of time and money)

Reason number six:

If you die first and leave everything to your spouse, you can make sure he doesn't leave it all to the new Mrs. Right.

Reason number five:

Once you get it done, odds are you won't die for a long time after.

Reason number four:

It will stop your spouse from his/her incessant nagging about getting it done.

Reason number three:

You can continue to control your money and loved ones from the grave!!!

Reason number two:

Peace of mind.

And the number one top reason for getting an estate plan done:

You can finally let your kids know, once and for all, which one of them was your favorite!

HOW TO PICK A GOOD ATTORNEY

FAMILY LAW

Most family law mediators will offer a free initial consultation if you are looking to retain them for your case. Remember that you will generally have to come with your spouse, at least to that first consultation, to avoid any conflict of interest or appearance of bias, which may otherwise arise if the mediator met with only one party. I give a half-hour consultation for prospective mediation clients, and should they choose not to retain me, there is no charge. During these consultations, we don't discuss the legal aspects of their case, but rather focus on the actual process of mediation and its benefits.

If you are consulting with a family law attorney not in their capacity as a mediator but rather to find out your rights, you'll probably be charged for the initial consultation.

In this case, the attorney is giving you valuable legal advice and will probably want to be compensated.

Unlike estate planning, where you will often pay a fixed fee, most family law attorneys or mediators will charge an hourly rate and ask for a retainer up front. It's very difficult, if not impossible, to know how much attorney time will be required for any given case. I have had very complex cases settle in our first session and very simple cases go on for - what seems like - ever. There is just no way to determine up front how quickly parties will come to an agreement. And in any event, it can be those "oh, our case is very simple and won't take long at all" cases that end up being the most complicated or taking the most time to settle.

ESTATE PLANNING

Because you really won't ever know if the attorney has done a good job in preparing your estate plan (think about that one for a minute...) you must rely on other factors in making your decision. Referrals from a trusted friend or financial professional are a good start. The local bar associations also have referral lists, but all this really means is that the practitioners are licensed to practice law in this state, they are probably not currently facing any disciplinary actions, and they have paid a hefty sum to be put on the list.

Once you find a prospective candidate, start by making an appointment for a consultation. Whether or not the consultation will be free may depend. For my practice, I offer a free consultation in the case where a potential client is interested in preparing an estate plan, currently does not have a plan in place, and is shopping around for an attorney. At that first meeting, we discuss goals, strategies and fees. I can usually quote a fixed fee at that time. For highly complex estates where the lawyer may not yet know the extent of the services needed, he/she may quote an hourly fee and request up front retainer. Be careful with open-ended retainers in this case. The fees may be justified depending on the level of work involved, but it may come as a shock at signing time.

In cases where you already have a trust and want an attorney to review it with you, this may be billed by the attorney at her hourly rate. Or if you are trustee of your deceased mom's estate, and have questions about how you are handling it - again, hourly rate. The distinction is generally whether or not the attorney is giving you valuable legal advice, which, after receiving it, you may not really need them anymore vs. consulting with you to determine whether you will want to retain them at all. The important thing, of course, is to know up front whether or not there is a fee for the consultation, so there will be no surprises when you get up to leave!

Also, at that initial consultation, the attorney should take enough time to get to know you and your estate, such that she can offer suggested plans, as well as guidance for some of the more important decisions you will have to make. My initial consultations for married couples are typically up to an hour and a half long. I get a general idea of their estate, their family members and their planning objectives. I also advise them on factors to consider in choosing trustees, guardians, continuing trusts and the overall type of trusts they can choose from. If the attorney can't be bothered to spend sufficient time with you at an initial consultation, odds are they will not be more generous with their time later on in the representation.

DISCLAIMER

So as not to disappoint my malpractice insurance carrier, (as well as any attorneys who happen to peruse these pages) I offer the following Disclaimer as any prudent lawyer would. Note that I have kept the font at a reasonable size despite the teachings of my Ethics, Counseling and Negotiations professor... So read on, intrepid warriors.

Disclaimer: This book is provided as a resource for general information for the public. The information in this book is not intended to serve as legal advice or as a guarantee, warranty or prediction regarding the outcome, suitability or applicability of any particular legal matter. The information is subject to change at any time and may be incomplete and/or may contain errors. Communication of information by this book (1) is not provided in the course of and does not create or constitute an attorney-client relationship, (2) is not intended as a solicitation, (3) is not intended to convey or constitute legal advice, and (4) is not a substitute for obtaining legal advice from a qualified attorney. You should not act upon any such information without first seeking qualified professional counsel on your specific matter. Any representation or warranty that might otherwise be implied is expressly disclaimed.

In no event shall Margaret A. Jones, Attorney at Law or its employees or agents be liable for any damages whatsoever, including, without limitation, incidental and consequential damages, lost profits or damages resulting from the availability, use, reliance on this book, whether based on warranty, contract, tort or any other legal theory, and whether or not Margaret A. Jones is advised of the possibility of such damages.

You agree to defend, indemnify and hold harmless Margaret A. Jones, Attorney at Law and its employees and agents from and against any claims, actions and demands, including, without limitation, reasonable legal and accounting fees resulting from your use of the material in this book or your breach of any of these terms and conditions.

Made in the USA
Monee, IL
08 November 2026

67378665R00080